Dark Matter

by

One of Many

Dark Matter

Copyright © 2020 by Ward Joseph Jarman

All rights reserved. No part of this book may be reproduced or transmitted in any form or by any means without written permission of the author.

ISBN 978-1-943424-58-0

LCCN 2019953600

About the Cover

At the age of fifteen the author was targeted by a Roman Catholic priest to whom he had confessed, many times, all of the sins with which a young boy struggles as he confronts his emerging puberty. A friendship grew which the author believed to be genuine but, as it turned out, was really just the grooming period employed by a sexual predator.

At age fifteen the author confided to this priest that he wanted to go with his brother and drink alcohol on a Friday or Saturday night when his brother and friends went out drinking. The author was disheartened because his brother always refused to take him. "I just want to see what it is like to be drunk," the young fifteen-year-old lamented to his priestly friend.

The priest responded to the youth that if that was all that was wanted, then he could take the youth to the priest's beach cottage and he would let the youth drink to his desire. On the designated weekend as planned, the priest drove the author to his cottage which was in another state, a significant distance from family and friends.

When the author finally reached a safe haven back at home, he went to the rectory of his parish and told another of his confessor priests about the traumatic experience and wanted to report the abusive priest to the police.

The response that he received was, "He (the predator priest) is a powerful man in the archdiocese. It will be your word against his. You will only be hurt again. I promise you that he will never bother you again and that he will never hurt any other boy again." The outcome of this brief conversation was that the author at fifteen believed this priest. The author never engaged in any therapy or counseling until 45 years later after he went into crises from reading about The Church's responses concerning the Boston, Massachusetts, child abuse scandal that was being reported by the Boston Globe. Specifically, the author was outraged at the feigning of shock and the statements that the Church was ignorant that this behavior was happening in the priestly community. The author new this was a lie because 45 years earlier he told the Church that this behavior was perpetrated upon him when he told his local priest about it.

The cover is the product of one of the therapeutic exercises during his years of getting professional help to cope with his childhood trauma. The author was given a plain white plastic face and instructed to make it represent the affect and effect of surviving his childhood sexual abuse.

Table of Contents

Dark Matter (Preface)…………………………………………………..2

Tension……………………………………………………………3

Hedgehog Empathy……………………………………………..4

Climbing: A Childhood Memory………………………………5

She Weeps……………………………………………………….6

Phantom Pain……………………………………………………..7

Brothers in Distress……………………………………………...10

Love Amid Abuse………………………………………………12

Seeing the Light…………………………………………………13

The Wedge………………………………………………………15

Leaf………………………………………………………………17

Banished to Oblivion……………………………………………18

Zombie…………………………………………………………..19

The Belt…………………………………………………………..21

Mother's Milk……………………………………………………23

Ugliness…………………………………………………………..25

Dance of the Iron Man…………………………………………27

The Mirage of Emancipated Consumerism…………………….29

Musing Over Dinner Alone……………………………………..34

Theology…………………………………………………………48

About the Author………………………………………………..50

Dark Matter (Preface)

I am among you.
Perhaps I'm a few,
but if I'm more then surely
you need to see the darkness in me.

Bright light floods through sparkling clean window panes
of youthful eyes awe struck with new life's ecstatic joy
to toy with adventure's luck, innocent of the human flaw
that calls souls to seek the meek weaker desirous prey
to feed the need to gorge on sweet tender freshness.

Dark matter is the hard crusted scabs of wounded visions of trust
betrayed by lust and power's need to be above accountability's creed to be just.

Dark matter is cataracts from stressful strains to regain youthful sight
amid the plight of progress for the few walled and gated from the neglected horde.

Accordingly bored with true equality
frailty is known as opportunity to dominate
and control one's fate to take more than is required
to stand higher above all others oblivious of their needs.

Tension

Empty stomach gurgling
moves keen predator to prey.

Gnashing dash slashing
Fleeing hope jumps to delay
The neck snapping fray.

Hedgehog Empathy

Oh that I could grow quills,
barbed and surgically sharp,

mini spikes of pain
to drain the enemy's blood,
to flood the floor red.

Tightly I curl nose to knees
squeezed into a fetal ball

protected, vicious,
a flesh slicing, razored sphere
of quivering fear

in tight young boy's white undies
that tease an old man's fingers

slick with blessed oil
wanting, needing, to coil
around virgin skin.

Holy art thou who speak not
to shame and refrain from aid.

I would if I could
lacerate his groping hands
and wash them in blood.

Climbing: A Childhood Memory

I squeezed as hard as I could squeeze
My arms around that big, fat tree
Unable to get a good grip.
I wanted to climb
Out of my shoes
Out of my dress
Out of my skin
Above and beyond
me.

She Weeps

Warm
   Moisture
      bursts
         through
            Membraned
               Love
                  . She Weeps.
           caressed
         tightly
        Embraces
      Loving
    is
   Happiness

Phantom Pain

The week was too long
Too strong with stress to keep straight
my gait to my goal.

Friday night's silent dark place
needs bright lights; boisterous noise.

I need song and dance
Libations to enhance chance
flirtations with smiles.

Off to Tom's Tavern's ruckus
to focus on gaiety

to share sympathy
with loyal friends' souls laid bare
to the week's torments.

Jamie's here with the others
A beauty marred, scared with loss --

a slim limb taken
from young perfect proportions.
Courage required.

Boldly forth we go to hold
true to our place in this race.

A beer for me, Tom
and whatever Jamie's drinking.
Run a long tab, please.

Pleasantries sent all around;
likewise reflected in kind.

Glasses clinked, hoisted,
emptied, re-ordered and sipped.
Off to the dance floor.

Jamie and I sit.
"How goes it with you?" I say.
"Fine. Work was busy."

"Are you in much pain?" I ask.
"You know it's funny; I feel

my leg still. It hurts
but in places not there.
Doctors tell me it's all normal."

Jamie left to relieve strain
gained from pain eased with fluid

transports to alter
hard realities made true
to undeserved youth.

Music and flickering lights
dissolved behind empty chairs

leaving me to stare
blankly dissolved from resolve
to relate freely.

Varied forms of quiet drinks
stink of medicative fumes

consumed by the sick
to be healed by learned men
who fight with demons,

microbes that attack the norm.
Damn the holy-man-disguise

donned by predators,
consumers of small boys' souls,
to fatten egos,

bloated spirits' infectious
need to breed poisoned child's dreams.

Brothers in Distress

My brother
and another
But not my brother,
hovers in ethereal shimmer
veiled in aborted memories.
Dead and Gone.

Bradley at 57, now William at 55,
derailed, assailed by unspoken torments
like desert sun rays scorching sweat beaded brows
wanting hydration for parched dried up souls,

Sought oases of green seen as a mirage housing cool refreshment.

The sucking pop of aluminum can ran through ear canals
as refreshing hopefulness to end harsh struggles

bubbled and fizzed froth of poured golden joy
down gullets of youthful desperation to succeed.

Drink up from an empty cup of fresh brew,
a malty, hoppy, intoxicant to keep minds ignorant.

Accolades gained and sought after fame
cannot tame the soul's need to believe in itself.

From the womb manifests dynamic potential undiscovered
unknown and shown only as warm throbbing vulnerability
that can shiver and wail in cold or coo in warmth
but can achieve neither independently.

You and I and all infants,
small increments to flourish or die,
rely on others' choices
to hoist upon us plenty
or empty our world of certainty
to see the next step to be the best me.

To feed upon the breast and rest upon her chest
Confidently free from fear and hear soothing sounds
surrounding my world with assurances
to grow and explore more than I know

Are gifts to lift the weak 'til strength and wisdom matures
into contours of muscle tissue from which issues
the force that cuts a course through the greedy horde
to score a secure place for new infants to grace.

But from the first small form to strong muscle and brain
is the exchange between us and the world of developed humans
who are predators of the weak, who seek all for their own,
who bemoan kindness and generosity as wrecking the gene pool
while hypocrisy used efficiently makes for dominance and supremacy.

Brothers in distress self-confessed in dark silence
their diminishing exuberance in their confidence
to heed the creed required to succeed.

Love Amid Abuse

A race to feel bliss
A kiss slipped between two lines
A missed step tumbles

like laughing child in summer
rolls over right shoulder once

to find feet
to pop upright to speed on
down green grassy hill

til before her shinning face
he stands on firm level land.

"Hi" and a bright smile.
She quickly presses soft lips
to touch his warm cheek

then she flees free abruptly
running ahead giggling.

My brief life with you
was blue sky and sunshine,
the eye of a storm.

Seeing the Light

Sulfur's stench beckons, 'Turn 'round'
as Hades' wisp waifs behind

gaunt, keen, scrapping limbs
whose face smirks contemptibly.
'Engage now or flee?'

A mouse scurries; a cat plays
Delighted by fright consumed.

Smoke's vagueness transmutes
into variegated fear,
sumptuous terror,

Cinematic, hyper-sensed,
Vivacious, heinous frenzy.

"Blood tongued demon
enmeshed in my mortal flesh
unable to free,

I see your oozing green eye.
I will stay your talon's grip,

Your pin needle probe,
Anxious for urbanite skin."
Virgin tissue throbs.

Charmed frailty heeds no loss;
Time scribes the demon's mark.

Acid etched groin bares
One, thin line hieroglyphic
Singed by Shiva's touch.

Melancholy's scar festers
Deep below congenial smiles.

The Wedge

In the quiet time
When all the world sleeps
creep to the kitchen;
seek your finest Sheffield.

From thick to thin,
The Wedge
will mark clean divisions.

Simple perfection
of a simple tool,
The Scalpel
will move apart skin layers
and tissue.
Move aside the ribs
and hold the beating heart.

Where lies my love?

From shaved head
glean the scalp,
cleave the skull,
gaze upon gray convolutions.

Where lies my soul?

Upon black velvet
lay the smooth brilliance
of dissected truth,
The point where western eyes curse

seppuku.

Leaf

Brittle brown leaf knocked,
Smacked, bumped, banged wind-creaked tree-bones.
Autumn's leaf – March wind.

Banished to Oblivion

Parental brutality
for the good cause
like strikes across the face
hastens maturity
but deforms the young soul
transformed in the anguish
of perceived disgust
and absolute
rejection.

As sons
I have come to believe
that we
survive the family tree --
you in denying
and I in defying.

Zombie

There is a darkness
in my heart
that stalks
like monsters under the bed,
ghouls in the closet.

A deep blackness
born from Mammoth Cave
without cold or heat.

Wide-eyed and blind,
no sense of space,
no smell,
no sound,
no air,
entombed alive,
surviving
the dull ache
of withered
emotions.

I cannot feel
yet I live.
Thinking
I surmise
to contemplate the righteous life
enthusiastically preached with passion
from childhood visions:

Towering
Cowering
in the corner
before Vengeance
I stood.

The crack to the face
of boyish hands in pockets
stings alive
protective postures.

"Put your hands down!"

Childhood obedience
Mystifies.

SMACK,
the second slap,
stings more.

At fifty-four
I feel
no rage.

The Belt

Brass and new leather
freshly stained medium brown,
lacing through dark loops

Is functional attire,
Unobtrusive Elegance,

for masculine wealth
in straight-legged, pinstriped suit,
Once Poverty's youth:

Sticks and stones, wild energy,
romping innocent ignorance

Folds that leather strap
(Push in to open its mouth,
Pull to crack a smack).

A woman's small, warm, soft hand
Lulls the male-child to sweet dreams.

Arise blazing son
Day's adventures are wanting
free flowing child's play.

Climb that mountain of knowledge
eight shelves high to the ceiling.

Beneath the wooden heap
of processed trees and bound leaves
blinks astonishment.

Anticipation lingers.
Reconstruction's completed.

Mother's eyes were brown
And the boy's buttock was white,
sumptuous beauty.
Unfastened Belt slid away
To reign in feminine touch.

 Tender flesh exposed
tightens beneath the swift sting
of hard learned lessons

And corporate mergers surge
From proper face and finesse.

Dress for subdued strength
with subtle accessories.
Always groom your belt.

Mother's Milk

Soft, warm, wailing flesh
Newly grown (five pounds and six)
wants a mother's milk.

Cradled support gently lifts
Dependency's needy lips.

"To my breast, my child
and suckle what is ours."
Sustained lives embrace.

Centuries pass in good grace.
We flourish unabated.

Cultivated mounds
Swell with vital sustenance
before steward hands.

Concrete dwellers civilize
into corporations.

Hail Los Angeles,
Detroit, Boston and New York,
Ancient tribes are gone.

Anemic, emphysemic,
Starving mothers have no milk.

Shriveled, dry females,
toxic crack and urban smog
(Hungry children race).

White sugar, energy's speed,
sustains no muscle nor bone.

Ancient libations
procuring Earth's pristine milk
eludes today's child.

Without a robust mother
How can Life's lust be sustained?

Ugliness

Cicadas are repulsive earth maggots,
Root sucking slimy protein secretions,
akin to globs of mucus, slugs or leeches.
Seventeen years of vile repugnancy worms through
the dark pitch of earth's fertile refuse
beneath the outreaching limbs of an aging tree
like so many boils spewing forth healing pus
morphs into red, bulging-eyed, lustful bugs.

In the yellow round space of a cast away bucket
small hands of tender flesh loosely packs a grass bed
to receive the unwilling guests that scavenging hands
have snatched and grabbed, nabbed in mid flight to frenzy.

Boyish giggles and a call to comrades, "come see how ugly!"
a pile of ugly, a brown, red-speckled, quivering mound of ugly.
Pre-K and K-feet, first grade feet, bigger bully feet, all race
to the place of captive oddities to spew the 'ew 'of delight
over the frightfully gross host of excitement.

> Scurry here; scurry there
> Catch the bugs in the air.
> Chase the girls in sweet curls
> With ugly bugs unfurled.
>
> Scurry here; scurry there
> Catch the bugs in the air.
>
> Eat'em quick, eat'em fast
> What a blast!

> Scurry here; scurry there
> Catch the bugs in the air.

A fair day for play with never-been-used displays
of pulsating life in bizarre bulges of bad noises.

Comrades called home by General Authority
peel away portions of ruckus energy
leaving a subdued trio
to gawk
at the yellow pit
of childhood sport.

A glint in the gleam of the eye twinkles with thought
that converts to huddled whispers fraught with newfound bliss
of childhood genius,
The nemesis of deformities and freaks.

The rubber snake, fluorescent green, poised its silver head
to expectorate the steady torrent of its liquid stream.

Into the mouth of the yellow cavern swirled a whirlpool of death
until overflowing
the world toppled over and flushed its bowel
in a flood
       down five
             concrete steps
                    to the street.

Curbside now resides a heap of childhood love.

Dance of the Iron Man

Hammer slams anvil
Iron to iron kisses
Flat, lipless, cold smacks.

Barren space between wants life,
soft flesh, a finger, to smash.

Test my life's metal;
Come down hard crashing cubed maul.
I bend with the blow.

Slow ascending, massive arm
Grows to bulge with more power.

Rise to your glory
Lift your bone crushing burden,
Servant of the Forge.

Linger at your full zenith
Savor your pleasure in work

in the lull I love.
From anvil to orange-white coals
Thrust my stiff resolve.

Fireball heat bathes my skin
Prostrated nude on boulders
beneath high noon sun
that sparkles on dark water
of the quarry's bed.

Molecular excitement
urges fluids to riot
with flesh wrapped in flesh
folded in mucus layers
to burst forth alive.

We are singed, sheared, cauterized,
Fused into a quivering goop,
melted resistance
spent atop hot island rock
Clutched in primal tongs
Plunged below frigid wetness
Shocked to congeal surface strength.

Lay me down once more.
Ring out the ping of impact
that flattens my joy

To deform my proportion
into a gleaming, sheer edge.

Razor sharp am I
That none can embrace but bleed
Tears for lost deceits.

Muscular, pounding biceps
Are naught but my self floggings.

The Mirage of Emancipated Consumerism

Every potential reality possible
regardless of rivalries
are seeds from the same source
without remorse for which course is taken
though human religiosity is shaken
as heretics are forsaken to the fire
hired to purge ignorance and evil.

Yet all potential realities possible
regardless of rivalries
are seeds from the same source.
Hyperbolic geometry or Euclidian,
Borellian logic and the con man's rhetoric
are known and therefore exist
to kiss my frail psyche
like the multi-faced street whore
looking to score my favor and coin.
Would that my groin could know better.

Cause-effect chains strain to explain
reductionists' pursuits to reveal truth
as plotted paths of chance enhanced
by adaptation to breed to exceed
the pack of mundane mass
of crass inferiors
doomed for extinction
beneath the expanse of superiors

whose true distinction
is to be the new mediocrity.

In Baltimore
The Lexington Market
bustles with its daily racket
of hucksters and consumers
swapping coins for fruit
or fish, roots and breads to suit
parameters of family pallets
ballots for weekly menus
that provide our cells 'energy revenues.

To eat the orange or the apple
to grapple with decisions of taste
for sweet potato or white
to bite into beef or sheep
or keep to the kingdom of plants
can't be excluded as trivial pursuits.
Yet selling your daughter
or your son
alters the enormity of choice.

The Greyhound bus
delivers girls without fuss
from its internal, narrow corridor
with labia-lip-like door
spread wide open before
the hard concrete floor
oiled and stained
while the night air remains obscured
blocked by pungent, carcinogenic exhaust
as small cost for diesel power at rest.

She emerges in pink sweater
with the better part of eighteen years
revered in new blue jeans
transported atop her sporty Nikes.
With suitcase in each hand
She stands as a brand, new, city commodity.

Runaways are best when they're fresh.

Yet predatory lust is ancient lore
born from male-female separation
under dominance over emancipation.

A quarter, a dime, a nickel, one copper penny:
Many bipedal hominoids dressed in tie and suit
comply with means to recruit more loot,
holy paper blandly painted with sacred ink
linking founding-father images with ether
worshiped as real matter
counted, sorted, catalogued and reported
then scattered among the populace
with purpose and intent to invent order.

Render unto Caesar as Caesar shall render unto you
the few
in favor
for support and homage to the demigod regime,
An ancient scheme of kings to keep barons
like harems from which to feed when in need.

Ladies attired in business, conservative blue
chew salad lunches and rue their days as kitchen slaves.
Male knaves who dug graves for female aspirations

to bury all assertions of self rule
school her to place and graceful servitude.
But some refused to be undone
and struggled in time to unbind their lives
to strive now among money changers and contenders.

Rebels, law abiders and kings in sheep's clothing
regardless of rivalries
are seeds from the same source
without remorse for which course is taken.
Disheveled beggar, repulsive trash picker
or beautiful youth disrobed on www dot expose_her
are from Plato's Socratic world of purity
hurled through human insecurity into imperfect reality.

Sweet, barely legal smile with braces
sighs and embraces the profiteering lens
with her brown eye defiant of shame
reliant on her firm, youthful form to gain
all that she needs and wants and more
to secure a domain apart from real chores
with fashionable apparel and regal cuisine.

But in this sensual scene of girlish flesh squirming
her first-harvest skin with round, brown-crested breasts
confirming her maidenly ability to consume
anyone's lustful flush
Is the slender, manicured, small hand
entering the framed foreplay array
of supple legs and cooing cries for partnership
without hardship while moistened fingers linger
 wooing internal tides of mounting tension by soft tissue touches.

"Feel the velvet pleasure," whispers motherly, gentle warmth.

"Let go.   Let go.   Let go.   Yes.   Yes.   Explode."

"A a a a a a h h h . . ."

Those manicured fingers stroked softly her wet beaded thighs.

"Well done my darling," directed motherly lips
as she kissed her foot wanting her praise.

Raise a toast to emancipated women
who boast their triumphs and just rewards
that afford them opportunities of equality
in a male world of commerce
immersed in procurement of currency.

Feminine lawyers and doctors,
senators and managers
of very young whores
Regardless of rivalries
are seeds from the same source
without remorse for which course is taken
For justice is never forsaken
and choice should not be mistaken
for freedom to succumb
to lower levels of evolution.

Musing Over Dinner Alone

Virgin fruit to jams consumed,
as Shiva's Tandava looms

over kitchen smells
of raspberry fruit preserved
then served or bartered

for parties or wrapped favors,
Waits quietly in cupboards.

Vacuum seal cracked, pops
beneath tight tops twisted hard
to yield soft spreads barred

from external corruption
of mangled fruits freshly crushed

and rushed to blue flame
that warms and simmers flavors
that must be savored

once spread on hot buttered bread
fed to sleepless souls wanting

nourishing delights
to relieve scratched skin's raw sting
sustained in Life's fights

to gain sustenance and clutch
much loved virgin existence.

Huge Hindu Himsa,
heavy in all human cells,
haunt food's pleasing smells.

The Universe that I am
moves through space and time confined

between finger tips,
head to toe, growing to know
undulating hips

equipped for merging bodies
into pools of viscous ooze.

I hunger and thirst
and curse the hearse that will come
when all days are done.

See the first light touch of lips
of teens who deem childhood trips

void of sustained joy.
Hours of skin explorations
win gentle sanctions

to pursue more stimulations
of biochemistry's creed

to breed and breed more
without heed to feed birthed needs
freed from woman's womb.

The Universe that I am
moves through space and time defined

by parental flaw
and biological law
enthralled with urges

to eat; nagged to satisfy
all unrequested surges

to pursue beauty
with hopes to copulate.
Yet imposed restraints

raise complaints of wenching woes
when yearnings fester below

surface smiles contrived
for polite, civil faces
that strive to survive.

Motherly wisdom given
to hidden woman waiting

in young girl's body
needing preparation's voice
to heed deeded truth:

"When money's scarce
The pantry's bare

So fair well, my dear,
and snare well a wealthy man
who will command strength

and power which he'll expand
for a grand security

for your sweet children,
their health and education;
their presentation

to the finest progeny
for their wedding remedy."

To my mind I find
the Universe that I am
moves through space and time

to be and see swirls hurled free
from constrained aims to govern.

When men expend their days
in crazed pursuit of women
consider closely

why war raged through every age.
High school fools review old rules

in sport and class
to sort the vast human mass
into the prized few

and the despised common horde
whose servitude is ensured

through well bred standards
of educated control,
high grades and good schools

which yield smart, dynastic jewels
to fuel the coffers of kings

who rule the State's wealth
for the health of the chosen,
smug Oligarchy.

Father's advice nicely said
to young boys bred to be men

will know how to show
strength, congeniality --
sincerity's face:

"Make no mistake don't forsake
cleverness, but speak clearly;

Deceive honestly.
All agendas are hidden.
Truth is forbidden

when seeking to win assets
to beset well dressed rivals

in the market place
of narcissistic finance
to enhance your life

with money and luxury
and every amenity

for dear wife and child.
Riled by poverty's ghost
a host of men scheme

and preen charity from soul
to shun street beggars unmarked

by tax break status.
Take care. Do likewise. Don't share
unless you can gain

advantage through civic pride
where many agendas hide.

Others are assured
with generational wealth
shamelessly amassed

then sheltered from tax and passed
to the detached, privileged few.

Son, don't be undone
by good deeds, but always be
very good indeed."

The Universe that I am
moves through space and time refined

by self reflections
tempered with imperfections,
driven by erections

of conceits to defeat myths
made to control pagan souls.

I hunger and thirst
and curse the hearse that will come
when all days are done,

But for now I'll eat slain meat
from the butchered cow cooked pink

and drink hearty wine
and dine under subdued light
alone with my muse

hopefully to be infused
with delightful new insights

into Life's function.
Breathing, the rhythmic heaving
of the human chest

can't rest from its given quest
to sync with the human heart

to oxygenate
my corpuscular transports
that infiltrate cells

to deliver nature's fuel
to burn star stuff's gruel

that formed what is me
and now earns energy's boon
from chewed nutrients

swallowed with intent and sent
down with tongue tickling tastes.

I live to consume.
I can consume only life.
Thus evolved this knife.

We are creatures of carbon,
Amino acid heads bred

by chance circumstances?
Random crashing and bashing
of stellar substance

fast fuses as consequence
if chance grants the circumstance

to form new atoms
to enrich this bedlam's odds
to prod more mutants.

But unstable elements
bent with their purpose corrode

to fizzle to death
or explode from tight tensions
wrenching apart bonds

of would be chance permanence
but for some performance based

cosmic conclusions
about solutions to support
and those not to court.

So, with my fine cutlery
polished nicely and sharpened

I contend with lust
for life to defeat and eat
to control and own.

Like the cosmic dark hole feeds
My lust receives all matter

trapped by influence
from solid, core confidence
and my pronouncements,

charm and cunning advancements,
prosperous entanglements

and well nurtured greed
that heeds nothing but this creed:
More matter and mass.

But what of your shining light
Muse of mine with bright, fair face?

I hunger and thirst
and curse the hearse that will come
when all days are done.

Must I listen to you, Muse?
What substance are you, really?

You say much, too much;
but confuse and flaunt pleasure.
You defuse my joy.

"Fair friend, eat your feast, drink wine,
dine in fine fashion. Don't speak.

Caution and passion
are not dire enemies.
See delicately.

Earthlings loyal to countries
can't see cosmic remedies

to ill favored gains
that constrain nature's movement
toward self improvement.

Your elements are star stuff
formed long before you were born.

First torn from The Core
in an explosive uproar
minute fragments soared

far to reality's edge
stretching Its new boundary

of infinity
finitely defined again
to extend beyond

Its known probabilities
to fresh possibilities

of future journeys
to embrace graceful wonders
or endure more grief.

A long circuitous path
of slamming and ramming parts

charts the aftermath
as bonded stability
or destined collapse.

This random hodgepodge display
is camouflaged persistence

that leads to green trees
from algae or land mammals
from pale amebas.

You and he and she and all
whom scientists call human

are past formations
of Future's new dominions
or fallen rubble

toppled from preset trouble
that's inherently coupled

with polarized bonds
binding desire and goals
with publicized roles

to be what's thought to be best
but hides your personal quest

to ingest and feed
beyond your need to exceed
any conceived threat.

Let us toast the host of change,
the spirit to rearrange

energy packets
stacked in crystal formation
as a foundation

for future combinations
that build more complex structures

first of passive mass
before primitive proteins
ooze forth from white ice

or liquefies from brown clouds
of toxins electrified.

Then consciousness blooms
as proteins transform to form
scribblers of strange runes

that hold thoughts fraught with wonder
about thunder and lightening

and dark shadow things
from down under that snatch souls
or brave, bold deeds told

to future youth caged in time
blind to the line that binds all.

Let's not curse the hearse
when all of your days are done
but toast the most change

for our self improvement
through our flawed involvement

with innate movement
to arrive only to leave
once we have survived."

The Universe that I am
moves through space and time defined

by parental flaw
and biological law
enthralled with urges.

Too much red wine when I dine
leads to empty, random rhymes.

I hunger and thirst.
I curse the hearse that will come
when my days are done.

Theology

Born in Western Civilization
I travel in hesitation to the East
in their thinking of The Way, The Tao,
How to live my life amid predators and prey.
Buddhism, Hinduism, Confucius and The Pope.
All offer hope to cope with loss and suffer one's cross to carry
to Calvary bravely to gain absolution from pain.

How can I refrain from distain for the Popes
who ruled the ordained shame of holy men's claim
upon little boys' innocence to be drained
under intoxication and humiliation
from slick probing fingers drenched in holy oil
consecrated to heal sick souls with tender touches?

Western Greeks' Socrates Speaks
Of searing light's cave shadows.

But the Yin and Yang
Merge light and dark's stark contrast.
Hence the pang of guilt.

A pure virtue void of vice
permeates Plato's advice.

But the East knows blows
on Shiva's drum and the hum
of the Tandava.

Disembodied Lucifer
At large, is my pain's main blame. ?

The relentless quest
to best challenge dark torments
rests with yin-yang tests.

In the breast of human flesh
resides the daily struggle
to abide by the light or hide in the dark
recesses of what we want over what might be right.

Contrite hearts may feign contrition to petition forgiveness
that they may remain unconstrained to reign
Under the cloak of the new moon night out of sight
to conspire and hire others of the same cloth.

Storms are congregating clouds
once white that block the sun's light.

In each and all souls
the yin-yang tension unfolds.
Dark there; Light must hold.

Seek not the disembodied
in conquest to best the other.

The power of good
is ours to wield to yield strength
with tensions controlled.

About the Author

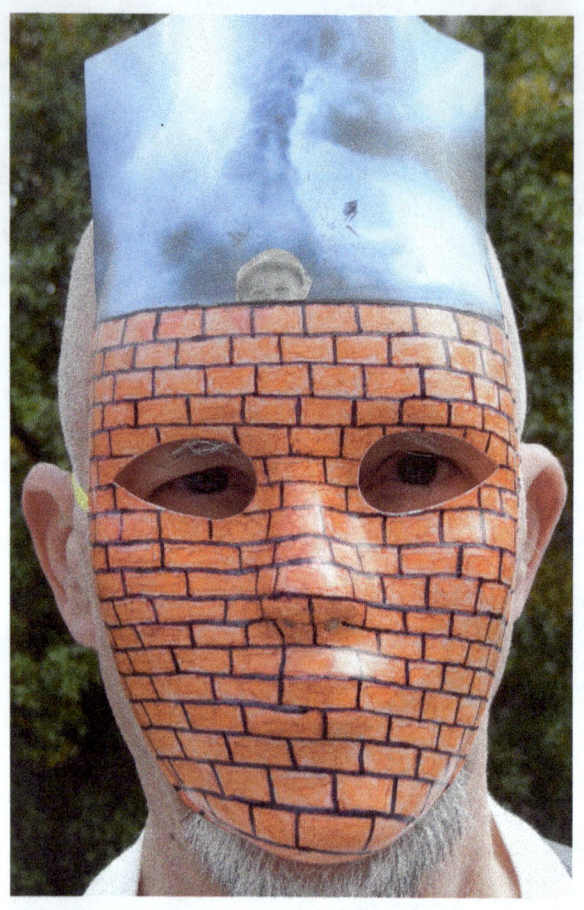

The author is an adult survivor of child sexual abuse. Sexual abuse in this context is not the legal definition, rather it connotes an adult predator targeting a child for sexual exploitation. The details of what occurred are withheld and frankly are none of anyone else's business.

One of Many

To clarify, I own the copyright to *Dark Matter* because I wrote it and it is a companion to *Deathbed Reflections* which also bares my copyright seal because I also authored that text. Instead of affixing "by Anonymous" I chose "by One of Many" because I am one of many adult survivors of child sexual abuse as well as childhood abuse in general. *Dark Matter* and *Deathbed Reflections* have arisen from one creative voice but that creative voice originates from a male who has experienced severe trauma in his childhood which fractured his self into pieces (ego states). Some ego states were not fully integrated with the others. One of these ego states was abandoned to lie suffering and buried alive in a very dark place to be ignored.

Two manuscripts authored by one voice of one person among many survivors represents and demonstrates the fracturing, disjointedness and need for reintegration necessary to survivors to regain wholeness. Thus the compelling motivation for both manuscripts to be authored by "One of Many."   Ward Joseph Jarman

www.ingramcontent.com/pod-product-compliance
Lightning Source LLC
LaVergne TN
LVHW061347060426
835512LV00012B/2594